FATHER FISHEYE

To John,

love,

Peter

Jeremy 1986

FATHER FISHEYE

poems by

Peter Balakian

The Sheep Meadow Press
New York City

ACKNOWLEDGMENTS

Grateful acknowledgment is made to the editors of the follow-
ing publications in which these poems have appeared: *The
Agni Review, Ararat, Carolina Quarterly, Chariton Review,
Confrontation, Colorado Quarterly, CutBank, Fresh Fruit,
The Greenfield Review, Hellcoal Review, The Nation, Poetry
Northwest, Poetry Now, The Remington Review, Southern
Poetry Review, Sou'wester, Three Rivers Poetry Journal,
West Branch, Whetstone, Wind,* and *Yankee.*

"Winter Revival," "Three Landscapes in Motion," "Poem
for a New Fish," "The Field of Poppies," "Reply from Wild-
erness Island," and "Homage to Hart Crane," first appeared
in *New Directions In Prose and Poetry 38,* (New Directions);
"The Blue Church" reprinted in *Anthology of American
Magazine Verse* (Monitor).

Published by The Sheep Meadow Press
New York, New York
Cover design by Cathy Aison; art by Ann Enkoji
Printed and manufactured in the United States
by The Studley Press, Inc., Dalton, Massachusetts
Distributed by Persea Books, 225 Lafayette Street,
New York 10012, New York

ISBN 0-935296-08-5 (cloth); 0-935296-09-3 (paper)
Library of Congress Catalog Card Number 79-90840
First printing

for my mother and father

Contents

Ocean Markings

Facing the Remains

The Busk

*"When a town celebrates the busk, they collect all their worn
out clothes which with all the remaining grain and other old
provisions they cast together into one common heap and con-
sume it with fire."*
        —WILLIAM BARTRAM, in *Walden*

This month has always ended with a mask,
the moon on a scarecrow in an empty field.
I come back this week before silage
is sealed. There are still green veins in the leaves
and strings of onion in the immediate yard.
This month every oak will go brown.
This month I'll tie hemlock to the fence,
refuse the faintest cricket, leave the suckle to dry
in the wind. This month trees
will be shrill without cicada.

I come back slow,
return down a road without gravel
while there is still a line of color
above the mountains,
and begin to admit what I have:
a square of earth frozen to my legs,
my blood with a small follicle of ice
pushing through my heart,
one arm scratched by the winding brier.

I come with the mud of the first planting,
one ankle still hairless from rain.
I bring the hyacinth we breathed in May,
the half-stem I found beneath your throat.
In my hand the first green tomato
that fell in the night.

I come back with a dogwood I found like a brush
in mid-August, a tree the sun would have turned
to smoke in another day.
In my hand the last petals of the hot roses
you picked in the morning.

In this field I throw a match
and watch the first smoke smolder beneath
the stalks and straw, hear the slow cringe of blue flame
spread along the stubble like a wave,
and with a wind, even a breath,
there's a white flame
that shows the trees big as they are
naked and shaking on the mountain.

Facing the Remains

I wake to tell you
cows have returned to the roadside,
the flax is like silk
around the ankles of planters.
I dreamt the carcass of our horse
picked clean by buzzards
glistened in the late sun.
The wind was yellow
and farms on the far slope
returned to shadow.
The hills were low and vacant;
light waned to a single line
and left us shivering to our thighs.

It was not the carcass
but the absence of birds
that left your hands limp.
If there had been one crow
to accuse, one distant vulture
circling in the haze,
I could have consoled you.
As it was, the two of us
stood there
in the late corn
motionless in the slow
night air.

Onion

Three weeks the autumn debris covered
the grass by the junipers.
Nothing could have lived under that lump of leaves
and brittle wood, the rotting and fungus.
The frost had come
rhododendron leaves curled
the soil beginning to firm.

Upturning sod first with rake
then with hands,
uncovering the underground kingdom,
the slugs, beetles, and earth bugs
making do on the underside of dried roots;
I dug through the smell of death
unplugging the light-stops and stones.

There seemed nothing but decay
everything for the garbage heap,
the earth on bottom bare—
all except for an onion stalk
flattened and curled
bare white at the base
yellowing at the tip
still giving off a small sweet smell.

Facing the Water

for Barbara

The tide ripples break over
rock and wash the anonymous
from below into the light.
Even the smallest turn and head
back into the dark where cold
is bottom. Where form shares
common ground with form.

Once more we face the water—
parentless, childless, gutting
ourselves of unspoken thoughts
          of bad dreams.

Two mornings I trolled the lakes
of Canada with your father.
The loons undisturbed by the noise
of the motor. We drank beer.
The run of the mill questions asked.
Who should succeed at what?

Two brothers of his never aspired
to anything. Twenty years later—
still town locals, they drink
coffee at Woolworths every morning.

This was further north than I
was used to. For a moment
the sun lay even with the lake.
The vinyl cushions were still
warm from our legs.

I could see the dug-up streets
of a Pennsylvania mining town:
houses crammed on ridges,
Catholic churches filled on Sunday
mornings. The Eucharist and
the glass breaking the sun.

The tracks laid for coal.
Coal in the air.
Coal in mountains behind the steeples,
coal in the arms of Slavic women.

There were no other words
spoken of you. I learned to cast.
The shady side, he said, is best —
keep the line away from the weed.

Mourning Robert Lowell

The trees begin to turn to wine
in Western Massachusetts.
The knot God made in Paradise
tightens on the hills.

Coming back to find Edwards
you bemoaned his relic oak
and knew the spider that set its web
in your heart before you left the Alps
still crawled the spokes of branches
you saw the sun drop through.

In the dark light of these slight
red trees, where Taylor sang off-key
and shivered, hasp on heart and mouth,
at the pettish wasp who caught
its leg in the center of the web

you left your insects for the test
in rotten hollow logs.

Your eye went red—
throbbed with these trees
in that late September morning dew
when tree to tree was stitched
with web too fine for eye to see
and spiders swam the air as sea
and disappeared in glisten.

This knot of veins and filament
your heart gave way before;
what kingfisher dived on your blue flame
and let you shake alone all night
before these trees had gone
from red to gray
and let the wind whine another winter
through their skin.

Edward Taylor in Late Fall

This world's all sky this time of year;
a rod of sun falls
through these trees
and makes their naked brilliant
gray shine more like foil
than my heart has known in spring.

In this time past all vermilion
oak and gold maple when hills
are rolling gray in empty branches,
this sun that burns the bark,
wells a fire beneath my feet,
sends a hot vine through my body

so whatever soil spewed fog
while the earth's sun rose
is now as dry as this morning's noon.

This Mountain That Once Shook Red

What fire in these trees
a month ago—
their limbs flamed
as if green were a solace
forgotten in the ash.

In dusk, they burned,
spit their blaze—
blurred the landscape
with a living blood

now the smallest branches
are thinning to the blue.

It's not the lessening of light
that slows my pace,
or the paling of sky
upon the hoary mountain

but, the way a buck
has to disappear beyond horizon
before he's out of sight—

It's because I know
I have to see
the web of all these branches
join the early dark
and leave the fattest crow
cawing in the air

that I hear
my own blood run.

This mountain that once shook
red, now turns
a cold slant of light
and burns this sky
so high and thin

geese seem faint specks
of black falling from the sun.

November Suite

1

This is the gray month.
Your breath is short.
Each morning the windows fog
from the low sky.
You picture a country
you've never been to
and think of the clouds
like cinderblocks
falling into canals.

2

On Election Day start
with a good breakfast.
Remind yourself, knowledge
comes in small packages.
The backs of colored boxes
keep your mind
off the temperature.
This month you'll need to eat
what's beneath the husk —
something for the skin to send
winter grass through the pores.

3

This is the week
your grandmother died,
you measure the age
of her skin by cambium.
Sell the bark to your mother
and she'll huddle under a tree
like a cold stray —
her freckles gone
for the first time.
The backdrop flatter than
the sky of a Byzantine painting.

4

On the third Sunday you'll
want to stay awake until
the light comes through the shade.
Tuck a small transistor
under your pillow to keep
the silence out of your ear.
You'll remember having done
the same thing the night Kennedy died.
Now, twelve years later
you learn to close the door.

5

The last Thursday will explain itself.
The distance between light
and dark shortens.
Sleep becomes a direction.
Geese prevent amnesia.
This is a sky that lets
light pass slowly.
Wake on this morning
and you'll hear sounds come
from the spaces between clouds.
You'll clip the buckle
on your boot, and feel
corn wilt the length of your back.
Chew on the stalk—
Let your girl make tea
with the root.

Winter Revival

Ice is imagined
as insulation from frostbite.
Gangrene is prevented
by the thighs.
Your tongue holds
the month,
curls the weather
with its vermicular
underlining
and returns heat
blue to the throat.

The night is exhaled.
Each breath
and another degree
approaches zero:
the center hard
with substance that moves
to fluid near light—
a circle with an ocean
frozen at bottom.

The white of the eye
has a light of its own.
You can even fish
its clear pool.
Drop the hook
beneath the thin
frozen lip
and wait patiently—
the line slipping
through your hands,
wind stinging your ears
crimson along a rim
of bony cartilage.

The flesh wrinkles
like hide,
hardens like the skin
of a lizard

even a knife-point
three inches deep
can only be seen
with the eyes.

Green Light/Perspective

One green light from the Christmas tree
cuts the branch of gray maple
travels to the fovea
and returns back through the window.
That's one theory:
if you let light out
into indefinite space
it finally returns to its source,
makes an equator
like a man lost on a freeway
in a car he has no control over.

This is a second:
the light from a Christmas bulb
travels through a fence
along the wire root of a rhododendron
under the top cover of snow.
If the fovea were larger
a green laser would flash
and return.

*

This is how I saw you
between shrub and window,
my eye good enough to follow
the weak light of phosphorescence
left by your tracks in the snow.

*

One less second of sun
and they would harden;
disappear from a distance,
leave me with a green bulb
slicing an angle of descent
on the far white slope.

Waking With Three Words

1

Trees make this light seem possible.
The same progression as yesterday:
black, a shade of blue, and a gray light
that changes the color of the eye.
A wing frozen between two branches —
the first crow you see brings snow to sight.
The closer the sparrow moves to shrubs,
the lower the mercury.
Rhododendrons tell the skin more than the eye knows.
Even the stem of ivy is frozen fragile as a cannula.

2

If squirrels surround the bark
and the sap turns hard,
keep the cat off the sill.
Whisper three Latin words to your lover,
no matter where she is.
Tell her you memorized them from a painting
by a Flemish Master, and that on a scroll
behind the Lamb these words were drawn
like fine thread.

3

Tell her that this morning
when even the apple in the Madonna's hand
would harden at top—
you'll exchange this simple message
for the way her hair sends this change in light
back through your eyes;
for the lining of her cheek.
Tell her that this morning
your arms are gutters
and three words are all you can manage;
that this kind of waking leaves
even the skin in the armpit blue.

For Susan in the Mountains

Your grandfather endured the ocean.
The trips back and forth
from Italy left him
hungry for good dirt—
a plot to lay the tomatoes
and some fence for the vine to climb.
When he fell from the scaffold
on the Comerford Theater,
they reset his hip
so that each walk he took
into the mountains sent the pin
through another black vein.
The creche, a cheap terra cotta
on your dresser
keeps the bloodline open
from the farm you imagine him working
to the olive of your arm.

*

Now the winter in Scranton
sneaks through the bad insulation.
The tomatoes, air tight
on your basement shelves
fight the ice with pulp.
The seeds you squeeze at night
come from what was red last summer.
Your lips like the pulp
make a water that is natural,
a water all their own.
There are no stems now, Susan,
and the night in Scranton
is blacker than slag heaps
sixteen year olds follow north
for cheap booze.

23

Your nails are chewed back
by this weather.
Your father's home at one again,
cursing your name.
Each mouth of hot whiskey
eating the brown edge of your eye.
Each time your name is called
the echo is louder, the walls harder.

Susan, February rain in Scranton
turns harder than cement.
The china your mother uses for tea
cracks from the ice
the gutters send up your veins.
She feels the kitchen steam
and your father's heat
run the length of her arms.

When she cries
the tomatoes sizzle,
and lose their place in the pulp.
The only madonna she knows
is on the tapestry
your grandfather lugged from Naples,
still hanging over her bed,
vigilant, waiting for a ship
to rise out of the ocean,
for the winter sun to come
through the coal.

Walking the Sun Down

The view from your window
is a town with one blinking light —
amber that is brighter
than the sun.
This morning each cloud clots
in your eye.
The wind widens your pupil
with a cold blast.
Somewhere eggs freeze
in the ovary of a hen.

Your first step into the day
loosens your arch.
Your bones could snap
like sticks with a wrong step.
You could draw cold blood
with each blade of grass
and long weed frozen like a needle.

Step into the wind
and walk the way
the cattails bend.
The air is cold enough
to make your sleepless night
seem like a dream.
You feel the wind tunnel
a passage through your ear
and realize you've been here before.

You've washed your hands
in this brook. Your skin
has been cut by this edge
of thin ice.
Winter fish have slipped
through your fingers,
the ones you catch
always oily and dark.

This morning you cook
your breakfast with a fire
kindled by your bones.
You hunch like a cat
in a white meadow —
the sun on your back
stiffens your fur.

You learn to use
the whole fish:
oil for heat, fin for direction,
and the eye to charm
the sun to a lighter shade.

Down the Cliff

for Bill Worth

You're back to Cambridge to weather
another Boston winter. Three years ago you left
with Kerouac's scripture in your bedroll
and a vision of a silent blue sky over the prairie.
I would have gone with you that fall
but what I had to learn led me to
the vacant lot next to our old grammar school,
the malls on Route 4, and the stools in the diner
where we once sat watching the grease sizzle
     in the dark morning.
I tried to tell you that winter, how I found Williams,
his grave half-buried in the swamp, his house
in Rutherford still yellow, only a hundred feet
from the drugstore.

Tonight is one of those nights when I try to
imagine the spring air driving the must
of winter away. It's a time in Jersey when the ice
is full of gravel and the asphalt breaks apart
and ruins even the shocks of jeeps.
We would take the road that wound down the cliff
and watch the dinghies and small outboards
brave the fog for carp and fluke.
Even when the fog lifted, the tops of midtown buildings
were hidden and the tugs were still a vague red
     against the gray.

These days it's hard to think about the future.
The vision goes horizontal, and the best of them—
Popeye, Crusader Rabbit, Rocky and his friend the moose
get mutilated by the blade of vertical band
that shoots across the screen. Even the backs
of cereal boxes are too thin to hide behind.
A plastic figure of your favorite centerfielder
for six boxtops and fifty cents. Who can afford
that kind of luxury? What I need these days is
an empty inlet, a horizon with a distant bridge
and a few unidentified birds.

A Sequence of Wind Between Seasons

Today is about forty and windy.
Trees sound like they are
breaking apart. Bark splinters
like the tearing of muscle.

There are more birds today
the ground is loosening.
The inside of the arch
loses its taut suspension.

The river gets greener
and the eyes turn furrows
in the bank. Life lost
at bottom rises, and the face
assumes a tint of moss,
a changing color of algae.

The body beats with the thunder
of birds. The body is where
a thousand swallows land and nest.
Grass, twig, and mud hold against
the wind, crows glean what is left.

Even the smallest animals
lose their thick fur
and use what remains from the first thaw.

The body finds holes in the ground
and fills with water. Twigs float
in the mouth. The eyes see eggs.

Birds find their way home.
No nests are ever abandoned.
The nose distills debris
presses its membrane to water,
the river returns
with tremble and a memory.

At the Grave of William Carlos Williams

This morning
I walk past your hospital
down streets you walked,
the babies still bawling
the Passaic piling garbage
on its banks,
the junk heaps fuming
in the meadow.

The plot of grass
I come to is matted
under a month's wind and snow.
The first crocus
packed tight inside a husk.

I bring no roses,
not even a daisy.
Only my hands
with the mud of March
deep under my nails,
and words from your wife
I found in the river.

Approaching the Summer Solstice

The Return

Your hair still blows
with the wind off the river.
Geese make arrows with
the sharp points of their wings
and spin the eyeball
through the gray to what we
once imagined as heaven.

The water is silent.
Any troller will tell you
how the current drags men
further downstream than fish.

You want to believe this river
has direction,
that small tributaries up north
empty into this wide span of gray water,
that there is a system
of xylem and phloem
beneath the bottom
that guides the water carefully
to a point where
gulls appear from behind black rock.

The sky swells
in one eye:
water in the other.
The moon fat with a full month
hides the tiny center
we think of as yolk
and sucks half our cheek out
from the bone beneath.

When you undress
yourself to this, remember:
the Amish farmer has patience,
a cold night in late April
leaves his beard a little longer.
He believes his tomatoes
have bloomed small yellow flowers
and will close to a white inside
they use for heat

the hex sign on his barn
rotates his wife's face
in a pattern that keeps
each season's sorcerer
beneath the corn.

Water for Land

for Jack Wheatcroft

An April wind turned a tricky current
and the hull hit shore. The brown slime
and sharp rock you slit the hard edge

of your heel on when you left, still there.
Wounds return this month. Bread unleavened.
Crocus split their husks in the earth.
Stony places lie inland, agony in your own garden.

The shore side of your house overgrown
with mulberry. The fence hidden behind
a blaze of forsythia.

Wet with flower,
dew still on your tongue and a scent
of stamen burning under nails

one foot on land, one in water,
the sun sinking out of sight—
You turn before the porchlight spots
your face and enter the sweet brine.

Poem for the Holy Week

This week begins with a sun small as a pin-prick.
Whatever drips hardens. A week of wind leaves
magnolia brown. In the morning news
Moslem guerrillas retreat from Beirut.
Last year's top pitcher holds out for a quarter million.
Up north trout are game for the first time,
the same tavern serves draught free till noon.

You think this morning the trout will bite hooks
and the same man will ride in the heat on an ass
accepting palms and welcome. The t.v. goes horizontal.
Darts catch the ten point rim. The record in the jukebox
is revised rock'n roll. The newsprint pictures
Bantu walking north for water. No camels
        in the background—
only a gray tone that must be sand and empty sky.

Rows of Tomatoes

Against the soil
wrinkled leaves

and the tough fiber of vine
surviving the wind

some frazzled
others dead at the stake

the earth open
yielding

we walk through
the smell of fodder

each step
sinking into the tilled clay

and your eyes
reminding me

of Van Goyen's mist
and mysterious sky
over a Dutch harbor

Here
the horizon clearing

a few patches of cloud
over the drying field

Approaching the Summer Solstice

for Helen

1

Stars have returned
to positions we're
familiar with.
This is night
when only beams
beneath the plaster
keep the sky
from breaking in.

Today we staked tomatoes.
The run-off from the river
has been good fertilizer.
The water gets deeper
and blacker with sun.
Reflection of form:
eyes, nose, shoulder, calf
return without a ripple.

Now the neighborhood idiot
prowls the banks
for young girls.
What is brown besides
your eyes
is a home for mollusks.

2

You'll wait for birds
or even light
to wrestle my arms loose
and tell me
you've dreamt me
back to water,
a scaleless creation,
slimy, eel-like
without vertebrae,
with eyes only large enough
to see shifts in light.

3

The season's without center;
too early for cicada
too late for tulip,
the rose still spinning
inside itself.

                    *

I come to ask why the heartwood
of the birch
tightens in the wind,
why on this edge of land
there is only a rubble of moss
and bent necks of weed
sucking water
from the center of rock.

I come to a point
close enough to see
the eye of a gull,
to an edge where the length
of my arms
and the span of my back
lose their measure
and the imaginary arc
between earth and sun
disappears.

4

The retina
finds the sharp rock,
the sea sends the sun
back through a choroid
and loses all current.

The pulse of heart
moves to the throat
expands to the jugular
and rises behind the eyes.

*

For a moment
even cormorants are still,
their foot scrawl
dissolving without a scratch.

I let water in,
take the sharpest shell
past the soft tissue.
I walk with a slow wind
and hear only names return —
a town, a woman
a bush that gives berries;
the sounds die three waves out.

In this air
flat rock glistens,
gulls swoop for fish
waves rise white off black;
my legs turn to weed

what I learn from the first fish
is how the fin yields
to a change of current,
how the color on the underside
reflects a tint of coral.

5

When there is wind again
land is not easy.
Flies crawl the dead crab
a weak wave cleans the last meat
from the mussel

algae change color
the first birds move
without sound

it's the inner ear that hears
the sand breathe.

43

6

This land is not as you said:
rocks jutting high above water
a sun turning the sea to a bed of diamonds
and one woman finding me
still on the sand,
foam sifting my flesh
back to bottom.

*

On this beach
the sun will be overhead soon;
bring enough vegetables for the long haul.
Bring the greens
that can stand the heat,
rhubarb because it grows
in sand
carrot and potato because they know
where the earth is cool
and can find water
without light.

7

I'll wake you before
my ears have recovered
from the pressure change,
before my eyes have returned
to white
and salt has left my neck.

*

In this moment before the eye
accepts darkness
and a wind through a low shrub
leaves the skin silent

I'll tell you that scales dissolve
at dark bottom
and return with coral in the shoal
and even a stream
the width of my foot
becomes a current.

Letting the Fog In

This morning I reach my hand out
the window and slice the air with the dull edge
of my finger. I lean my neck through
the window pane for the sound of a bird
and lose the sound of my own heart.

I want to gather this air
in both arms, hug it
to my belly and bring it to you

I would let it away slowly
so it would creep between your toes
and swirl your thin ankle.

I would watch it broaden over your thighs,
funnel to your hip, and spread the width
of your back. When it rose over the nape
of your neck and your eyes became dim light

I would assure you that outside
this fog rises from puddles,
trees are shortened
red brick disappears
and headlights spoke the air silver.

I would open the window the width of my finger
and let this white morning take me by the neck

and assure you pine needles flicker,
the edges of leaves dissolve like their roots
and several birds cheep far off.

Loving in the Corn

Across your face this green hangs limp.
The thread of light that breaks your hair
brings back the tint of red age has hidden
and dies along this base of stalk.
There's no slight husk with filament of silk,
no joint with cob to point us back to light
or high tassle to catch the sun at peak.

If cows collapse from heat we'll not hear
an echo or a wail, just this dim hissing
of roots that brings your back to curve,
returns this furrow to one dark space
between ourselves. A month's heat rises
through your legs up my blue-root veins
and disappears in a wind that drops
from whisper to breath.

Portrait Before Water

You remember the day you were born.
June. Superstition: a myth
of snow and gray Friday pass
through back villages you imagine
abandoned by your grandmother
when the Turks knocked down
the front door. You hear the oracle
and pretend your mother's a whore
you knew from Brooklyn before
your testicles returned their veins
blue to your hands.
You refuse tears and settle
for bad laughter because the last mirror
you looked in sent back a portrait of you
at sixteen in cut-off shorts
flexing your left triceps
into a clean harbor.

No boats flouted your voice.
No seaweed stood between you
and the reflection of your body
showing veins in the forearm.
Schools of fish slithered the length
of your arm with care,
lined the shore-edge of your forehead
and disappeared into deep green.
Even crab that caged the rock
kept their claws from your eyes.

When your eyes left your face
in a countercurrent
you refused to admit the pain.
You turned away and left without them
making believe the sockets
you carried in their place
could send the sun back
to water without nerve or lid.

As Brancusi Said at an Earlier Hour

for Doug Bennett

I never made it back to that bar
in Elmira where you and that thug Fitzie
used to end weekends in rage.
Where you crowned your girl with broken
glass and washed the body from
your hands. Every mirror broken
and still your face whole in each frame.
And that last headpiece you made from
rusted lead. They believed you'd pillage
every town from Elmira to the border
and disappear into the North wood
waiting for the second coming.

They say you were unrecognizable.
Steel twisted around your arms,
handlebars locked around your head.
When I went back, your room still
stunk of clay and wet cloth.
Nothing untouched. Beer cans
in the toilet and that selfless
portrait without eyes dug into the plaster.
Everything was still except one woman
on the sill, your hand half-pulled
from her head and her eyes
still waiting for you to attack them.

Thinking of Cesar Vallejo in Late July

You know the way he died;
early in October on a rainy Thursday
in Paris.
That is a way I do not want to go.

This man who knew the sun on a flat roof
and the luxury of straw,
who knew the hair on his shoulders
the way he knew the lowest roots in his garden.

Why then in Paris in October in the rain
with nothing but a concourse
and nineteenth century statues by his side?

If I can believe for one moment that on that morning
in the light stillness of his room
he saw the black eyes of the woman he left in Lima,
and that through the street noise
he heard his mother telling him to eat,
to eat the tails of shrimp and knobs of squash,

If I can believe that his father remained as vague light
in a field of wheat,
and he heard him through the wind saying,
"I accept your words, I will not read your letters
to my wife,"

then I will walk out on this day in July
without a thing in my hand or a person in my heart
and know this dawn oozing green
is my only way of going.

Relief

If you return the room will be empty
as in mid-winter.
Mold will begin to scent the corners.
Dust from the sills will leave
a fine silica over your arm hair.

By ten, the sun softens the honeysuckle.
You smell the vinyl on the seats,
work the sweat from the steering wheel
into your palm. On the radio the score
of last night's game you missed;
home team loses in extras on errors,
bullpen shows signs of August.
Maybe this morning a relief pitcher
wakes on cinder behind the outfield fence
asking the score.

The window sends back only sun.
A vine climbs the drain-pipe.
It was yesterday you clipped a rose
and ran a petal the length of her back.
It's easy this morning, without wind,
to hear the cicada in the veins of your neck.
That way even though the glare of the windshield
makes the pines lose their angular shape
and the needles their fine points —
the trees seem closer.

You know if you go back, you'll take
even the jar with leaves floating in it.

Late August Sequence

1 *Empty Barrel*

This begins in dry brush,
cicada and tired honeysuckle.
Crows without seed
in the dead vine you lug
home each night.

You stalk the ground.
Apples over outgrown root,
dog manure and flies.
Mosquitos half-mad
gyrate in clusters.
A shadow moves like an animal
over grass.

2 *The Attic*

Twenty-five days without rain.
Your arms dry as the earth
legs motionless as yellowing grass.
The body sheds the light
and moves back to bottom like a slug.

The late rose breaks apart.
Not one petal left to hide in.

This morning no light
through the shade.
You curl beneath the quilt,
your flesh gone;
and listen to the wind
blowing through the attic
slamming the trap door open and shut.

3 Open Window

In a wind, the sky breaks,
birds lose their sense
and the air thickens.

You hear a rabbit scud over fence board
for the hollow side of an oak —
the empty baskets blown into the picket.

Even the smallest inch worm
curled on a thread hears it.
The smallest bud knotted under bark
moves closer to the light.

The Fishing Trip

"The penis is the bridge."
—Norman O. Brown

for Bruce Smith

A man drives off, four-thirty
with only birds to remind him of his escape.
He thinks of his wife's back rising and falling
with each breath. He imagines she has passed
the deep stages of sleep and is returning to dream:
fish swimming in fountains, naked statues with genitals
large as arms, her father refinishing chairs in Vermont.
He sees his own breath in a gray line from his nose
and knows that on this day, before he's kissed
an inch of flesh, this line defines his face to the world.

*

Coffee's a breakfast on a morning like this.
He tucks a thermos between his legs and the aluminum
uncoils the hair on his thighs.
A man hides behind poles and tackle, net and bait.
Sure, he tells himself, there'll be a lake,
some bass and perch, carp if nothing else,
maybe even a glitter of fin along the cutbank.
The radio comes in loud from New York,
the same songs every half-hour; the lyrics reminding him
of what he's doing, of how the same sounds repeat
the same skips, of how a man lives by the story
of his own fishing trip
until he believes he's caught the hook on his palm.

*

By eight there's nothing more than road
and static. In a few minutes his wife's dreams will end.
She'll wake not knowing how the rain hammered
the windshield before the sun rose. She'll grease
a frying pan thinking his catch big, imagining large fins
flapping his forearms.
At nine he crosses the state line.
There's a diner with night truckers and cops
coffee and danish. He finds the bathroom,
unzips by the machine selling prophylactics and combs,
pulls his penis out and lets it wriggle like a new worm.

Poem for a New Fish

From Solstice
a Pentecost is past.
The sun's movement visible
once more from a position
fixed in the mind.
The sun
if it rotates in your sleep
still recedes
to a single point
where the earth's
open eye
becomes your own.
The arc you draw
from a shore point
is the azimuth
marked by the pupil.

In a week there will
be more undertow,
the small bones
in the foot will bow.
You can almost predict
the flight
of the albatross
over the antarctic —
the span of wing
over ice.
Each wave diminishing
with the size
of your pupil,
the water dropping
to where your ankles
leave the air.

*

Let your foot
follow the current.
The thin membrane
of jellyfish
will widen the pores.
Imagine yourself sinking
into the den of China,
admit that the sand
packs the memory
hard to the heel-skin,
the minimal arch bunches
the unknown to a cold
bone, the rest passes
through a fearless tibia.

Salt dries
on your leg hair,
a calendar drops
from a plane
flying advertising.
The ocean dissolves
all the waste
you can imagine.
Last night you came
here to piss,
dropped your trunks
and let the salt
find its way
through the pubic hair
to your skin.
Your penis wriggled
like a fish just hatched,
the salt water washed
the inland dryness
out of your bowels.

China was itself again
and the moon
August orange
spoked a light
a hop, skip
and a jump
to a vanishing point
beyond your arm.

Rowing Home

after Winslow Homer

Home:
the sun holds
the scene in place.
There is need of
strong current
and wave —
for oars to join
with arms
and bring the eyes
back to where
the sun makes sense.

From a point
where cloud opens
on the azimuth,
a sun dangles
like a foreign object
caught in the pupil.
The lid can neither
close on its rim
nor look into
its red center.

To organize
this sky means:
clouds will move
swiftly north
and three men
will bring
the sculls
back to the sinew
and pretend
their wives
are black rock
on the distant horizon.

60

Ocean Markings

Words for My Grandmother

Today the azaleas bend
rhododendron leaves curl and brown.
The trees are bare
with remains of leaves
and abandoned nests.
Small swarms of birds
break, dive, and rotate
in a cloudless sky.
Once more November
shortens the light.

My body tightens,
makes its way through
leaf piles turned humus
and debris soaked by the night's rain;
spaces between earth and sky
cloud, field, and stone
you too once entered.

It is ten years since
you last saw your breath
in a November air,
and these shadows
moving with day
across the base of this oak

ten years to a night
I last walked
your dark stairway,
water hissing on the stove,
your orientals worn
and beaten into deep
reds and blues by your
half-confessed past.

63

When you took my head
in your arms
and kissed my hair
I stared as always
for a moment
at the skin of your hands
still discolored by
the arid Turkish plain.

The History of Armenia

Last night
my grandmother returned
in the brown dress
and high black shoes
standing on Oraton Parkway
where we used to walk
and watch the highway
being dug out.
She stood against
a backdrop of steam hammers
and bulldozers,
a bag of fruit
in her hand,
the wind blowing
through her eyes.

I was running
toward her
in a drizzle
with the morning paper.
When I told her
I was hungry—
she said,
in the grocery store
a man is standing
to his ankles in blood,
the babies in East Orange
have disappeared
maybe eaten by
the machinery
on this long road.

When I asked for my mother —
she said, gone,
all gone.
The girls went for soda,
maybe the Coke was bad
the candy sour.
This morning the beds
are empty; water off,
the toilets dry.
When I went to the garden
for squash
only stump was there,
when I went to clip
parsley
only a hole.

We walked past piles
of gray cinder and cement
trucks, there were no men.
She said Grandpa left
in the morning
in the dark;
he had pants to press
for the firemen of
East Orange.
They called him
in the middle of night,
West Orange was burning
Montclair was burning
Bloomfield and Newark
were gone.

One woman carried
the arms of her child
to East Orange last night
and fell on her uncle's
stoop, two boys came
with the skin
of their legs
in their pockets
and turned themselves in
to local officials;
this morning sun
is red and spreading.

If I go to sleep
tonight, she said,
the ceiling will open
and bodies will fall
from clouds. *Yavrey*
where is the angel,
where is the angel
without sword, *yavrey*
where is the angel
without six fingers
and a missing leg
where is the angel
with the news that the river
is coming back,
the angel with the word
that the water will be clear
and have fish.

Grandpa is pressing
pants, they came for him
before the birds were up—
he left without shoes
or tie, without shirt
or suspenders.
It was quiet
the birds, the birds
were still sleeping.

The Blue Church

(after L'Eglise d'Auvers *by Van Gogh)*

The windows are deep blue
as the sky.
The woman who walks
down the left fork
of the road that branches
at the church door
is hunched like a cow.

Blue shadows spot the road.
The clock is faceless,
the bell tower silent
with blue wind
winding through the shutters.

The sky turns dark
on the horizon.
The woman who walks
toward the trees
sees the flowers go black
one by one,
and the orange tile
on the far barn
turn to sky.

Three Museum Offerings

for my aunt Gladys

1

This crucifixion made from cottonwood
gnarls at the base.
The pain is in the grain of wood.
The feet twist where the root was pulled
from the ground.
A crown of thorns from brier, ruddled
and twined around the head.

In certain towns in the Southwest
a woman dressed as death
danced for three days
before falling to her feet
at the foot of this cross.

*

Accept the rib I remove from his chest.
They stirred red ochre with it
to paint the woman's bones
and then returned it to its place
on the cross.

2

This wooden mask
kept winter out of the Eskimos' blood.
The hue of green around the eyes
kept the face from disappearing into snow.

When a woman came to the shaman
with her sick child,
he stalked the tundra for twenty days
and wandered out over hard water.
When he returned with ovaries of fish,
seals reappeared and the Kuskowin broke open.

*

Accept this shell that covered
his cheekbone, and this piece of mouth
blushed and open.

3

This spear weathered and white was used
by Indians of the Plains to drain and cut.
It bled bad dreams, delirium, and ghosts.

When a mother came from her sleep in fever,
two infants strapped to her legs,
the skin of her parents in ash;
the medicine man slit her arm
and drank blood.

*

Accept this bone handle worn and smooth
and this chip of slate that is red.
It still cuts skin.

The Field of Poppies

for Lu

Cypress spiral to the sky.
Painters came here because
the dirt was dry as their bones,
because even the monastery on the hill
flaked each day.
You want a picture of yourself
in this poppy field;
wind blowing the long grass
around your legs,
fields of yellow flower across
the road moving away from you.
The high mountain is where
the town's saint disappeared
with his wound.
When he returned
peach trees sprouted from rock,
and the gray clouds left the mountain.

Cypress spiral to the sky.
Your father found this field
and the mountain uncovered,
the monastery a pure glint of sun.
You want this picture
to show your body disappearing
in the red waves of flower,
a field of pin-pricks
rising and falling in the breeze,
each step spreading the red
over your joints.

You want the red to cover
the mountain,
you want the line where
sky and land meet
to turn the color of the heart.
This is how your father left;
foot, knee, stomach, face
disappearing in the stain of this field,
in the light wind that sang
in the red flowers.

Ocean Markings/The New Year

for aunt Lucille

Everything's frozen to bottom;
scallop shells ridged in place
the spine of each sanddollar split,
small August drift like iron
on the jetty.
Each wave that breaks on shore
returns nothing.

You come back to this,
to the level of ocean
and find gulls white as ice
scanning the low tide.
You hear the wind slam
the doors of empty bathhouses.
The hedge that bloomed tiger-lily
now winds like capillary around the rail.
Even the grease from May's Drive-In is dead.

Tonight you'll let the shadow
of your mother hobbling along the wall
return to sand.
You'll come and lay the bones of your father
in the last imprint of the crab,
and return the eyes of your sister
to the pearl white shells
that know the deep weed beyond the jetty.

If you stare into the loud black waves
that claim and reclaim the moonlit rows of shells
emptied of their meat,
you'll hear the sound of birds
too far off to be familiar.
Think of their wings poised in the wind
making a long silent arc
against the furious air.

Three Landscapes in Motion

It happens like this:
a sagging willow brushes
the top of your head.
The ground like a strange
foil shines.
You move by waist
through high grass.

You take the dry weeds
and use them for arms.

*

A stream thinner than your wrist
dries at your feet.
Red clay cracks
like the skin
of the lizard's lips.
The sun withers to
an orange arm.
You want to follow it out

you remember
the other side of sky
is cold as the rock
that sends a breeze
to your face.

*

It happens like this:
sky lowers to your ears,
you find the bay
entering your mouth.
Small bait and weed
run the passage of your nose
and return to wave.

You recognize the far shore
as a wide belly of fish —
the near jetty
as black fin.

The Angler

The angler who first spoke of net and line
hook and spear, who saw the first fish turn
from scale to fur and move on land,
knew what Ambrose, who swallowed more sea
than his Father would give him, meant when he said:

Sweet flower of fish I know your way,
I know the ship of wind that plucks your scale
of flower, I know the lily neck of froth
that strokes your long fin.
What I want is the black bottom that matches
your eye at dead center, to retrieve what I've given,
give back what I've lent.

This ditch that I fish from while the sun falls away
knows my ankles and my spear
knows the tremble of my knee when the night
is all but here and the water
takes the weed back from my net.

Reply from Wilderness Island

I want the eye of the fish to turn
in the black water
and catch the sun of my hook.

For the fish enters my dream with
a smooth fin for my face.

*

I want the tail of the fish
to turn inside my muscle
and travel my spine as it would the rushing stream.

For the fish enters my dream
with a sheen of scales changing in the light.

*

I want the fin of the fish to wriggle
its fine web in the dark center of my chest
turning all blood from water to a pool that covers rock.

For the fish enters my dream
with green gills and a ruby-stained belly.

Night-Catch

There's nothing for the hands to claim,
this trawler's back from red sun
fishless, wet fins in his eyes.

His net shines once more
like gossamer in early dew,
the light dies through it

more slowly than a trawler's
bones can hope for, or a far
warehouse with empty panes lets happen.

The sun shrinks to a cataract eye,
goes black beyond some cave
he looped at noon,

and returns his arms to spray
and the net to lapping tide.

Fishing Off the Dark Rocks

I'm here on the knife-point of the jetty
where brine and once clear brook-trickle join.
There's been no sun for days,
every nook that's not too black and deep
is slime, my pole is slime
my palms, part clam part brown moss,
let the thread go lax, drop a wide arc from rod
as if the ocean floor were all mouth
and vulva swallowing my sore torso slowly
so I might confess, my feet wet with night,
that I'd rather be bot, slug, or snail
than stand this reeling toothless crone
whose body is all hole beneath each flittering wave.

Wind Vespers at Narragansett Bay

When low clouds dim to dark bush
and light returns to a spare line
beyond all factories and ships
and each dock goes back to black skeleton,
there's an air that begins
in the eye center of a pit
inside my wind-strung chest.

The bay turns its breath to breeze,
gray waves churn a suds that finds
my bones, spills a pulse that is all rush
and turns all heaving air
back to bottom where voice begins.

Homage to Hart Crane

This morning kelp is drying on the dockside,
women leave the laundromat early.
I walk the low bank
in the low air
and feel the long bones in the river's belly
hiss in the warming water.
How many warmings of current wound through
your eyes Hart Crane?
This morning your dry rib
passes this juncture of ocean and calm.
Here where there's no bridge
and gulls roost on tied barges
and skim the black harbor for carp,
your marrow goes the way of slow mollusks.

The sun moves
in a steady progression upwards
to a point
for a fraction of light
before it starts to fall
and here, Hart Crane
even the falling warehouses
look like cathedrals for a moment.

This morning a drunken fisherman
wakes on cinder with dead bait in his hand,
not knowing the day of week
the month or year,
not knowing anything
but the spot he sees the sun in,
the noon wind riveting his ribs.

It's a good thing, Hart Crane
that I'm baitless and hookless
that I leave the bay without a fish,
my net shredded and hanging on the old post
        at the South Dock.
It's a good thing my girl took the first train south
and that this noon I unwrap my sandwich alone
under the empty elm, with three birds singing in my ears
and the cats meowing over empty clam shells
        and shrimp husks.

What luck Hart Crane
that I came this morning to feel your one bone
dragging along the bottom
just as the sun was climbing to the top
and the fisherman was waking,
just as the tugs were disappearing
and the barges were settling in
to the winter lapping of the harbor,
just as the cod heads were softening around the eye
so the gulls could snap them up.

"My Mother Is a Fish"

—FAULKNER

My mother is a fish
and the sky is low and orange,
the long grass rises
in the still air.
The mud is black
and the worms turn
their cold segments
at my feet.

> I used to walk
> with an old lady.
> It seemed far from water
> and the ground sunk,
> the weeds were higher
> than my head,
> the fat worms were
> always lying on top
> half asleep in the mud.

My mother is a fish
and there is a low sky
that swallows my head,
a fine rain
comes as the night leaves —
a field that dries
in the spring slowly
because I am a worm
purple and headless
in the cold mud.

*

In March before the crocus
and the lily
there are eggs in the shoal
in the green jelly.
The crab glides backward
and doesn't see them,
the kingfisher falls in the wind
and lands on his head in the sand.

I used to bring him
a bucket of shells
and old codheads
for his neck.

At night my mother is a long
eel with a light
winding around the rocks
off shore.
Even without a moon
the land is not black then
and the rocks glow.

*

The sun grows like an egg
over the bridge,
the first birds are silver
and swoon down for my mother.

> When the lady came
> we jumped —
> She took us to find worms,
> worms we could squeeze
> in our hands.
> There might be a fish
> at the bottom
> I could squeeze
> with my hands.

I went with my father
in the dark water,
I went with a bucket of mud.
When we doubled the worm
on the hook
and it coiled,
I went limp for the cod
and the bass in the mud.

When there was a fish
I would grab it
with a wet hand
and take it to the bottom
of the bucket;
its eye going black
in the middle of air.

You must hack it
along the green gill
and throw the head back
to the gulls, he'd say.
Watch the eye disappear
on the waves,
watch the belly
rise its last time
in my hand before the sun
falls on the water.

*

My mother is a fish
and flutters in my bucket.
the sky is a fleck of stones
over the night water

and turns my arms silver,
sends a wind that calls
my father out
to where the bigger birds
dip and rise,
call, and caw, and spin,
on the far water

where my father goes
and leaves me
with the mud
where the gulls
glide and lower
with my mother in the belly,
with my net and the worms
and my arms going silver.

Father Fisheye

The sun is gray and without a rim,
what light there is the water catches and keeps.
Fishmongers bear the crossed keys of the saint
on their arms. St. Christopher lived on the gulf
and sang for the kingfish when the winds left,
let his arms out from their joints when the old men
left in the dark with their trawl.

Father Fisheye, I come here to the rocks where the fires
are all ash, where the dockmen have disappeared
for the day of Gennaro and the boys with straw hats
have left with their fathers' empty creel and sandworms
in their pockets, where old men still sit staring
at the short ripples that go white at their feet.

I come to this inlet for eels and crabs
for gangs of minnows that move like a long tail
and turn silver in the gray sun.
Father Fisheye, the air is still, trees motionless
the sky touches my chest.
The sun is lost in the gray dusk water, gone into gullets
of fishes that wander slowly out to the far waves.